Lifestyle-integrated Functional Exercise (LiFE) program to prevent falls

Trainer's manual

Lindy Clemson, Jo Munro & Maria Fiatarone Singh

SYDNEY UNIVERSITY PRESS

Published by SYDNEY UNIVERSITY PRESS

© Sydney University Press 2014

© Lindy Clemson, Jo Munro and Maria Fiatarone Singh 2014

Faculty of Health Sciences, The University of Sydney

Reproduction and Communication for other purposes

Sydney University Press
Fisher Library F03
University of Sydney NSW 2006
AUSTRALIA
Email: sup.info@sydney.edu.au

National Library of Australia Cataloguing-in-Publication Data

Author: Clemson, Lindy, author.
Title: Lifestyle-integrated Functional Exercise (LiFE) program to prevent falls: trainer's manual / Lindy Clemson, Jo Munro & Maria Fiatarone Singh.
ISBN: 9781743320372 (pbk)
Notes: Includes index.
Subjects: Lifestyle-integrated Functional Exercise (Program).
            Falls (Accidents)--Prevention--Popular works.
            Exercise--Popular works.
            Physical fitness--Popular works.
Other Authors/Contributors:
            Munro, Joanne, author. Singh, Maria, author.
Dewey Number:
            613.0438

Cover design by Miguel Yamin

The Lifestyle-integrated Functional Exercise (LiFE) program to prevent falls has been proven effective in reducing the risk of falls and in improving capacity for functional everyday activity. Balance and strength, particularly ankle strength, can be markedly improved and maintained if the LiFE program becomes part of daily routines.

The LiFE activities have all been designed to help you keep active and reduce your chance of falling.

The program was developed and piloted as part of a University of Sydney Bridging Grant and the program was tested in a randomised trial funded by a National Health & Medical Research project grant ID 402682. The results of this trial were published in the *British Medical Journal*, 2012. See section on 'References' on page 89 for full bibliographic details.

We acknowledge the contribution to manual development by Anita Bundy and Trish O'Loughlin and the other therapists of the LiFE research project.

We would also like to thank the team from the University of Wisconsin, Madison and the Aspirus group in Wausau for their assistance, feedback and suggestions regarding the trainer's manual.

Contents

Introduction

Introduction

Welcome to the LiFE trainer's manual.

If you are reading this manual you will potentially be training people to do the LiFE program.

All the information in the trainer's manual is relevant and important to be able to effectively train participants. The sections are presented in an order that follows a logical pattern. However, you do not need to read from front to back.

What is LiFE?

The Lifestyle-integrated Functional Exercise (LiFE) program to prevent falls is unique and novel. LiFE involves teaching core underlying principles of balance and strength training. These principles form the basis for the balance activities and strength activities used in the program. The participant makes changes to how they perform their daily tasks to include these activities. That is, they embed the activities into their daily tasks and routines. Eventually the changes become a habit that is going to improve the balance and strength of the participant.

The participant and therapist plan how to embed these activities into the participant's daily routine. No two participants will have exactly the same program as it will be determined by what the participant routinely does and how they decide to embed the activities into their individual routine.

LiFE was developed in response to a need to provide options that are acceptable to older people and are sustainable over the long term. To develop the balance and strength training we drew on programs such as Helping Elders Activate their Lives (HEAL) (Fiatarone Singh & Murphy, 2003) and evidence for effective falls prevention to devise our core principles and strategies. Our belief was that functional-based activity will closely align to skills needed to prevent falls and improve the participant's capacity to recover from loss of balance or tripping.

The concept of balance training or the notion that you can improve your balance is not easily understood. Yet there are many opportunities in daily life to challenge balance and load the muscles to make them work harder. LiFE incorporates an understanding of these principles and provides many examples that can be incorporated into the activities of daily life.

What does LiFE do?

The aim of the LiFE program is to reduce falls and improve functioning in older people by embedding activities that improve their balance and strength into the participant's daily tasks and routine.

Participants need to continuously challenge their balance and make their muscles work harder. In the LiFE program the balance and strength activities are incorporated into their daily tasks. This is why it is called a Lifestyle-integrated and Functional Exercise program.

Who is LiFE for?

The LiFE program is for anyone who is at risk of falling. Participants must be able to comprehend the program and not have a cognitive impairment. They must be able to safely perform the LiFE activities unsupervised. They should not have a neurological condition that affects their balance. Although the participants in the research had two falls in the past year or one injurious fall which they self-reported, this program is not just for those who have already experienced a fall – it is aimed at the prevention of falls.

Who can offer the LiFE program?

A LiFE trainer needs to understand the key elements of the program, how to implement these for each individual and how the activities will benefit the person undertaking them.

To be a successful LiFE trainer you need to:

- have a belief that it is possible to improve strength and balance in older people and that this will have a direct impact on protection from falls and improved function
- understand the LiFE principles of balance and strength training and be able to teach these to participants
- understand the seven balance and seven strength activities and be able to teach people how to incorporate these into their daily tasks and routines
- be able to provide effective feedback and motivation to participants
- work with concepts of habit-change to enable participants to implement and sustain LiFE activities
- Be able to assist participants to become autonomous in implementing the activity program.

In our research we have had occupational therapists, physiotherapists and exercise physiologists teaching the LiFE program.

Before teaching the program therapists need to:

- read thoroughly the LiFE participant's manual (*Lifestyle-integrated Functional Exercise (LiFE) program to prevent falls: participant's manual*)

- practice the activities in the participant manual themselves

- spend time implementing the program into their own daily routine

- understand how to complete the assessments used for the LiFE program

- understand how to complete and appreciate the importance of the recording sheets that accompany the program.

It is strongly recommended that before teaching the program therapists and trainers implement the LiFE program, or significant sections of it, into their own routines.

Each participant will need their own copy of *Lifestyle-integrated Functional Exercise (LiFE) program to prevent falls: participant's manual*. The participant's manual includes the principles, activities, tips, photos and ideas on how to include the balance and strength activities into the activities of daily life. Throughout this trainer's manual we will refer to information that can be found in the participant's manual.

> **LiFE is different to traditional exercise programs. Some therapists may need to 'get out of their therapist hat'. Therapists need to let participants decide when and where they will do the LiFE activities. The activities are not taught as a set in one place; instead, you need to move about the participant's home and enviroment. Therapists and participants together work out different LiFE activities that suit different places. It is a more facilitative process.**

Key points of the program

Participants will learn the LiFE balance training and muscle strengthening principles and activities that relate to these principles. They will then learn how to embed specific balance and strength activities into their daily tasks and routines.

To improve their balance participants will need to practice activities that challenge their balance and keep progressing to more challenging balance activities.

To improve their strength participants will need to make their muscles work harder by loading their muscles.

Participants will:

- learn to look for opportunities in their daily tasks and routines where they can include or embed the balance and strength activities
- need to practice to make it part of their usual routine
- change their habits to include balance and strength activities into their everyday tasks
- learn how to make the exercise program more effective by making changes to their environment that will encourage them to do more physical activity.

The program will make it easier for the participants to become more physically active.

> **Safety must always be a priority.**

What is functional exercise?

We generally think of exercise as specific set of activities that is performed separately to the other daily tasks and activities that we do. Many people find it difficult to find the time to do the activities that may be beneficial to them. Incorporating the exercise into routine daily functions, tasks or routines means that the daily task becomes the exercise. This may lead to a greater success rate in achieving strength and balance improvements.

For example, we know that doing squats will improve the strength of the quadriceps muscles. Stronger quadriceps muscles may assist in preventing falls. In a regular strengthening program participants might do 10 to 30 squats three times per week. Many people find full squats difficult or aggravating to their knees. However, if people are able to think about bending their knees in a half squat every time they had to reach below waist height they may achieve a large number of these every day with less risk of aggravation of any knee problems. Participants will be incorporating an activity that will improve their strength into their daily function. This is what we mean by functional exercise. It is NOT a rigid set of activities which must be performed for a set number of repetitions at set number of times each day for a set number of days each week. The number and type of exercise that each participant will do will depend on their lifestyle.

Why activities and not exercises?

Throughout the program we refer to balance and strength *activities* and not exercises. This is to reinforce the idea that the program is not a set of exercises in the traditional sense, but balance and strength activities that are designed to be embedded into the daily tasks and routines of the participants. Participants will be changing their habits. They may be changing their environment. Ultimately, they will be making changes to their lifestyle that will impact positively on their strength and balance and ultimately help prevent falls and in many instances improve their ability to function.

By the end of the program participants should be able to:

- perform the balance and strength activities in the LiFE program independently, safely and competently
- embed LiFE balance and strength activities into their daily routines and tasks
- upgrade the balance and strength activities independently and safely
- increase their physical activity.

Expectations of / for participants

Participants need to:

- be prepared to make changes to their lives
- practice the activities independently
- read the manual and refer to it regularly and as needed
- look for opportunities to embed the activities into their daily routine
- complete the recording sheets
- become autonomous in implementing the program.

It is not expected that participants will understand everything at the first training session. There is a lot of information to absorb. The program is about changing habits, which is a slow process. It may take a number of sessions for the concepts, principles and activities to become familiar to the participant.

Over the course of the program the participant needs to increasingly take ownership of planning and implementing LiFE activities, guided by the therapist. Enhancing self-efficacy and habit formation are key concepts within the training. We recommend reading the article by Lally and Gardner (Lally & Gardner, 2011), which provides a nice overview of habit-formation theory and evidence to date.

About the program and implementation

- It is an individual program tailored specifically to the lifestyle of the participant.

- The therapist teaches the program and facilitates the implementation by creating a set of balance and strength activities that the participant performs independently by embedding these activities into their daily tasks and routines.

- The program is taught in the participant's home and their own environment.

- The number of sessions is based on the participant being able to learn and integrate two balance and two strength activities each week.

- Some participants may not be able to learn two balance and two strength activities each week. Sessions 6 and 7 can be used as needed to ensure all activities can be taught. These final sessions can also be used to reinforce the activities or upgrade activities or to address any problems that may have been encountered.

- The teaching sessions are carried out over an eight- to twelve-week period with the participant gradually increasing their autonomy in upgrading and sustaining the embedded balance and strength activities.

LiFE is taught in five home visits with two booster visits and two phone calls. It is taught with consideration for:

- the correct performance of balance and strength activities. For example, keeping trunk straight when moving to limits of stability and taking care of back posture.

- safety. For example, having safe support readily available, not doing LiFE activities when wearing unsafe shoes, being aware of obstacles and good lighting, and responding to potential hazards by ceasing LiFE activity.

- matching prescribed LiFE activities to individual capacity

- choosing tasks and routines that are relevant to the participant

- increasing intensity, upgrading over time

- frequency, which is as often as the participant can. LiFE activities should be done multiple times throughout the day. Be creative about ways to increase the number of times through changing things such as where and when each activity is embedded.

Table 1: overview of how to implement the LiFE program.

Session and week number	What the therapist needs to do	Time allocated
Before sessions	• Send participant the *Lifestyle-integrated Functional Exercise (LiFE) program to prevent falls: participant's manual* as well as the Daily Routine Chart (DRC) and instructions on how to complete it	
Session 1 Week 1	• Evaluate ability and opportunities for LiFE activities (LiFE Assessment Tool [LAT] and Daily Routine Chart [DRC]). • Introduce the LiFE program and go through the participant's manual. • Commence teaching the LiFE program – key points and balance and strength training principles. • Teach and implement one to two balance and one to two strength activities linked to a specific daily task, situation or place. • Plan how, when and where to embed the activities and record the plans using the Activity Planner. • Plan activities to be counted using the Activity Counter. • Instruct participant how to use the Activity Planner and Activity Counter.	1.5 hours
Session 2–5 Weeks 2–6	• Continue teaching and implementing the LiFE program. • Introduce and teach new activities – one to two balance and one to two strength activities each session, linking the activities to specific daily tasks, situations or places. • Increase the autonomy of participant in selecting opportunities to embed activities in daily tasks and in upgrading. • Use the Activity Planner to record plans and upgrades. • Use the Activity Counter to provide baselines and reinforcement. • Teach ways of making the program more effective.	1 hour each
Sessions 6 and 7 Weeks 8–12	• Finish teaching the LiFE program if not completed. • Review and encourage activity upgrades. • Encourage continued integration into daily tasks and sustaining habit change.	1 hour each
Phone calls 10 weeks / 5 months	• Provide support and encouragement. • Address problems if they are present.	

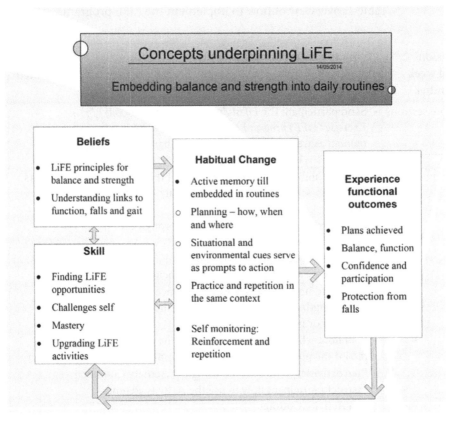

Figure 1: concepts underpinning LiFE.

Figure 1 provides a framework for LiFE summarising the main concepts underpinning how to embed balance and strength activities into daily life. This includes features that enhance beliefs, attitudes and understanding of the program, strategies to encourage habitual change, and the positive functional outcomes that sustain engagement in the program. These latter include prevention of falls, increased function and greater participation in activities and life roles. This framework and its importance is discussed in this chapter.

LiFE: an evidence-based program

LiFE was first tested in a pilot trial, the results of which were published in 2010 in the *Australian Occupational Therapy Journal* (Clemson et al., 2010). This first sample comprised 34 community-residing older people, aged 70 years and over, who had either had two falls in the past year, or one injurious fall. They were randomised into either the LiFE program or into a no-intervention control group and followed for six months. LiFE significantly reduced falls by 77% (IRR=0.23 (95%CI 0.07 to 0.83)) in this small exploratory study. This led to securing funding from the National Health and Medical Research Council for a large trial.

The results of this major trial were published in 2012 in the *British Medical Journal* (Clemson et al., 2012). In this three-arm trial we compared LiFE to a sham exercise program and also to a structured exercise program, once again recruiting people who had either had two falls in the previous year or one injurious fall. After a twelve-month follow up there was a 31% significant reduction in rate of falls (IRR=0.69) for the LiFE participants compared to a comparison group who received a sham exercise program. The structured program (balance and strength exercises three times a week) showed reduced falls but there was not a significant difference compared to the control group.

Recruitment strategies included mailed invitations to people 70 and over using medical practice and departmental databases. A letter was sent letting them know about the opportunity to be part of the research and that we were recruiting people who had had a fall in the past year. We asked them to telephone or respond by mail if they wanted more information. The Short Portable Mental Status Questionnaire was used to screen people for cognitive impairment. Further information on the research procedures can be found in the open-access article available from the *British Medical Journal* (Clemson et al., 2012).

Table 2: balance, strength and confidence findings, a three-arm RCT (Clemson et al., 2012).

	LiFE v's Control	effect size	Structured v's Control	effect size
Timed tandem walk	F=6.6 P = 0.002	0.42	F = 8.9 P<.0001	0.49
Balance hierarchy scale (8 level)	OR 1.5, wald 15.6 P<.0001	0.63	NS	0.29
R Ankle Strength	F=5.5 P=.005	0.40	NS	0.26
Balance confidence	F=5.52 P=.004	0.38	F=5.22 P=.006	0.37

Tables 2 and 3 summarise some of the findings of the LiFE program compared to the structured program. For the LiFE program, there were significant and moderate effect sizes for both static balance and dynamic balance and for balance confidence. For LiFE, while there were steady improvements for hip and knee strength, ankle strength was the only strength measure to show a significant effect. LiFE demonstrated moderate to large effect sizes in measures of function and daily activity and in a measure of participation (see Table 2). Adherence was sustained with 64% still engaged in LiFE activities at 12 months.

Table 3: measures of function and participation. Comparing LiFE and structured programs with a control group (Clemson et al., 2012).

	LiFE v's Control	effect size	Structured v's Control	effect size
Timed tandem walk	F=6.6 P = 0.002	0.42	F = 8.9 P<.0001	0.49
Balance hierarchy scale (8 level)	OR 1.5, wald 15.6 P<.0001	0.63	NS	0.29
R Ankle Strength	F=5.5 P=.005	0.40	NS	0.26
Balance confidence	F=5.52 P=.004	0.38	F=5.22 P=.006	0.37

The strong outcomes of the balance, function and participation measures suggest there is a range of benefits to the LiFE program. The program differs from structured traditional exercise which is performed in measured doses and in discrete sets. Many of the LiFE activities align with functional conditions and everyday tasks and they are encouraged to be done as often as opportunities arise. There is emerging interest in the beneficial effects of short bursts of exercise.

Other aspects of the LiFE program may enhance generalizability to protect against a fall. Because of the embedded nature of LiFE activities, activities often include dual tasking, that is, completing more than one task at one time. Research suggests that dual task training can have a positive impact on gait stride, gait variability and balance (Silsupadol et al., 2009).

Not just balance and strength

Functional activities, not traditional exercise

While our evidence shows we did have physiological improvements it may be that the reason for enhanced benefit for LiFE is that it is a functional exercise program. By embedding LiFE activities in daily life, the person is automatically placed in situations of competing demands. This connects balance and strength training to daily living tasks which naturally add challenging demands. This can include, for example, selectively paying attention to the environment around them as well as dual tasking as they are doing the LiFE activity.

Balance challenges when dual tasking can have a functional benefit

LiFE activities often involve tasks that require multiple skills to be used at the same time. This is often referred to as dual tasking as the tasks involve varying combinations of physical movement and upper and lower limb coordination, as well as attention to the task at hand. Examples of dual tasking include a one-legged stand whilst ironing, or squatting rather than bending in the supermarket when selecting items from a lower shelf.

Having a poor capacity to perform dual tasking in tasks that involve gait variation and demand attention has been shown to predict an increasing risk of falls (Kuptniratsaikul et al., 2011). This risk is increased for repeat fallers (Beauchet et al., 2008). Training in dual-task activities that challenge balance in clinic situations has been shown to improve gait stride and variability and dynamic and static balance (Silsupadol et al., 2009). LiFE has shown this can be done in everyday situations and that these skills transfer to other functional tasks. It may be that the tailored and embedded activities of LiFE enhance the integration of skills such as task coordination, postural control and spatial processing.

Activities involving planning, concentration and attention

Activities that involve planning, concentration, attention and strategising could have a direct impact on falls prevention (Liu-Ambrose, Ahamed, Graf, Feldman, & Robinovitch, 2008). Think of what is involved in challenging balance when talking on the phone, carrying things whilst turning or going up stairs or tandem walking down the hall carrying a cup of tea. Liu-Ambrose et al. (2012) propose that it is not just physiological improvements that can be gained from exercise but that executive function and functional plasticity can improve from targeted exercise. They draw on understandings of brain function, evidence from their own and others' work in resistance training, and on studies exploring the relationship between fallers' performance on tasks that demand attention and tasks involving executive function (Anstey, 2008). They assert that, along with physiological change, such mechanisms may play an important role in how exercise reduces falls risk.

Concepts underpinning the LiFE program

The LiFE program is different to a traditional exercise program and may require a shift in thinking or focus for therapists. As therapists we look for ways of making tasks *easier* for our clients or of having them do *less*. The LiFE program encourages participants to look for ways of doing *more*. Activities which challenge their balance and strength are incorporated into daily tasks and routines.

These activities are linked to specific daily tasks. They are performed intentionally and consciously until they become habitual and embedded in daily occupation. Feedback, monitoring and positive reinforcement are strategies used to enhance skill in the performance of the activities and the self-efficacy of the participants.

There are concepts that underpin the implementation of the LiFE program that are vital to understand. These are:

1. embedding activities into daily routine
2. changing habits
3. challenging the participant.

1. Embedding activities into daily routine

In LiFE participants do balance and strength activities while undertaking their usual daily routines and tasks rather than doing these exercises as a separate set of actions. They perform the activities multiple times each day by incorporating or embedding them into a variety of tasks throughout the day. The activities are done intermittently and often. These activities are based on the principles of balance and strength training.

For example, unloading the dishwasher becomes an opportunity for the participant to strengthen their knees by doing multiple partial knee bends. They still get the dishwasher unloaded and also complete their knee-strengthening activity. The activity or exercise becomes part of their daily functioning. This is why it has been called a functional exercise program.

The focus is on choosing safe activities which are relevant to the individual and upgrading these activities over time. Starting levels are determined by thorough assessment using a specific tool designed for the LiFE program. The implementation of the activities is done collaboratively with the participant. The therapist works with the participant to help determine how and where they can embed the activities safely.

Upgrading of activities is initially closely monitored by the therapist. However, the participant must ultimately understand how to upgrade their activities so that they can continue to challenge themselves when the therapist intervention has ceased. This gives the participants more control over their program than more traditional exercise programs.

To effectively embed the LiFE activities into their daily routine the participants will need to develop new habits.

2. Changing habits

Participants in the program learn to change the way they perform certain daily tasks to include LiFE balance and strength activities. They will form new ways of doing tasks as part of their habitual routine. Therapists need to facilitate this habit change by providing strategies that transition the novel activity into a routine part of the daily task. That is, LiFE activities need to become habitual. When the activities become habitual they are more likely to be sustained.

The process of habit change is built into the implementation strategies for the program and includes the following:

a) planning and visualisation

b) cues to prompt action

c) practice, repetition and reinforcement.

a. Planning and visualisation: how, when and where the activities are to be implemented

Holland et al. (2006) stated that planning and visualising changes were important because they helped formulate the intent to action and acted to strengthen the association between the situation or environment and the action. They demonstrated this through the example of how the conscious planning of activities was the key to changing recycling habits in a workplace.

Participants in the LiFE program are expected to plan when and where they will perform the activities and to which of their daily tasks they will link the activity. This is documented on the Activity Planner. They should visualise themselves performing the activity while doing the daily task. The particular task then becomes the cue for remembering to do the LiFE activity. For example, a participant could practice tandem standing while washing up; then doing the washing up becomes the cue to do the tandem stand.

In the longer term we want participants to generalise the activity performance to other contexts. We want them to be able to transfer the activities to as many tasks and places as possible through their daily routine. When they have mastered the skill of performing the desired activity embedded in a specific daily task, and are doing this routinely, they should then try to visualise themselves performing it in other daily tasks. They can plan to embed the activity in the new task in addition to the former task.

For example, they might start with bending their knees to get the detergent from below the sink. Then they plan and visualise themselves bending their knees in the bathroom to get the toothpaste out of the cupboard or in the kitchen when getting the plates out for dinner.

Visualisation is a strategy to assist planning where the activities can and will be embedded. It is also assists participants generalise the activities to a variety of tasks and places. Recording how, when and where on the Activity Planner is important but it is the visualising and planning that are the key features of this process (Holland et al., 2006; Lally & Gardner, 2011).

A planned commitment to a behavioural response occurs within a particular situation and in response to a particular cue. The ability to replace old habits with new ones is dependent on both conscious planning and the influence of situational cues (Holland et al., 2006; Lally & Gardner, 2011).

b. Cues to prompt action: behavioural, situational and environmental

Changing behaviour requires prompts to elicit the desired behaviour. In LiFE we have used a few different methods of providing the cues to prompt the desired behaviour. There are general prompts that apply to all participants. These include bending your knees if you need to reach for anything below waist height or go on your toes if reaching above waist height.

To facilitate the embedding process the participants plan which daily tasks the LiFE activities will be linked to or embedded within. These tasks then become the situational cues to prompt the performance of the LiFE activity. Situational cues can be a place and time, for example, the kitchen sink in the morning; a feature of the environment, for example, the doorway between the hall and the bathroom; or a pattern of interaction with the environment, for example standing in the supermarket line. These cues act as a prompt to elicit the behavioural response – the performance of the LiFE activity.

The program encourages participants to make changes to their environment to facilitate the performance of the LiFE activity such as moving commonly used items to a different place to promote the performance of the LiFE activity. For example, moving the detergent to a lower shelf to prompt knee bends; moving the tea cups to a higher shelf to prompt toe raises.

The aim is to have participants performing the strength and balance activities without having to consciously think about including them in their daily tasks. This way, they become habitual. However, while learning the program during the training phase participants must consciously think about the activities and embed them into daily tasks, that is bringing them into consciousness or active memory. We learn new habits by incrementally processing over time using our active (or procedural) memory. Over time they become habitual and automatically embedded in daily occupation. Habits are routine, goal-directed behaviours that are set in motion by situational cues (Ronis, Yates, & Kirscht, 1989). These can be automatic and may even go unnoticed or may be intentional where the situation needs to prompt us to action.

Changing habits requires time. This is why training in the LiFE program is done over a six- to twelve-week period. LiFE requires working with active memory until the activity becomes a stable and enduring habit, and is embedded in routine. This is facilitated by practice and repetition in the same context.

c. Practice, repetition and reinforcement

Planning and practice are both critical in implementing new habits. Participants have to plan to do the activity, visualise themselves doing the activity then practice doing the activity consciously and repeatedly until it becomes habit.

When a new action is performed, a mental association between situation and action is created, and repetition reinforces and establishes this association in memory (Lally & Gardner, 2011). Participants should complete recording sheets to reinforce the practice and repetition of the LiFE activities in their daily tasks. These recording sheets provide an opportunity for participants to plan when and where they will embed and perform specific LiFE activities, whether they were able to embed the activities and how often they were able to embed the activities. Completing the recording sheets reinforces the performance of the desired activities. For further information see the section on 'Planning and recording performance of the LiFE activities'.

Therapists provide extrinsic reinforcement for the performance of the activity by reinforcing any level of performance, but always encouraging performance of more, either additional activities or a more challenging performance of the same activity.

Participants gain intrinsic reinforcement for the performance of the activities in a variety of ways. For some it is seeing that they are able to do more of the LiFE activities by reviewing their recording sheets or because they realise that they are able to perform the activity at a more challenging level. For some it is the ability to perform a daily task more easily or more confidently. For example, many participants felt more confident in their ability to climb stairs.

Reinforcement from therapists is important during the initial phase of training. However, the intrinsic rewards provide more long-term reinforcement of the activity performance. Therapists need to facilitate habit changes. This includes helping participants plan the changes, visualise how and when they can embed the activities, demonstrate the activities and provide opportunity for participants to practice and provide feedback and positive reinforcement.

Practice and repetition is crucial to habit formation. The article by Lally and Gardner (2013) which we recommend provides a good overview of the stages of habit formed in a similar context each day. So rather that planning too many different contexts you might start with bending your knees instead of bending at the waist every time you close a drawer in the bedroom and kitchen. Once habits are formed this can be generalised to broader contexts such as the supermarket, the garage or other places that the participant goes.

The Activity Planner is designed to reinforce the performance and embedding of the LiFE activities. The planner includes prompts to link the activity with a daily task and provides participants with a method of recording whether they have performed the activity or not, and how often they were able to perform the activity. The process of recording draws attention to the achievement and reinforces the performance of the activities. The Activity Planner and instructions on how to use it are in the section on 'Planning and recording performance of the LiFE activities'.

Throughout the training phase, the autonomy of participants should be facilitated to enable them to continue implementing the program independently.

3. Challenging the participant: mastery and upgrading activities

The concepts of challenging oneself, mastery and upgrading are interconnected. They are all important skills that underpin the LiFE program. They all refer to the idea that participants should continue to challenge themselves by continuously upgrading the level of activity they undertake for balance and strength activities.

To improve and continue to improve balance a person will need to practice challenging balance activities. To improve strength a person has to continue to load their muscles and continue increasing the load on their muscles.

To continuously upgrade their activities the participant needs to be able to set a goal related to a LiFE activity, determine when they have mastered that activity or achieved the goal, and then set a new, more challenging goal. Self-efficacy refers to the perception of one's ability to reach a specific goal (Bandura, 1997). Increased self-efficacy is likely to improve the outcomes of the program as the person has a stronger belief in their ability to perform and achieve. The ability to set realistic, short-term, achievable goals as well as mastering an activity can increase the participant's beliefs about self-efficacy when they prove that they can master the activity.

Mastery refers to the ability to perform an activity at a certain level. Inherent in this concept is the idea that new challenges can always be created once a particular challenge has been overcome. Mastering a skill involves breaking it down into simple and manageable steps and having incremental goals working towards achieving these steps. In the LiFE program participants have to master an activity at a lower level before they can safely progress to a more challenging activity. As participants master an activity they have to be able to set a new goal. For example, when a participant can stand on one leg with two-hand support the participant then sets the goal to try to move to a one-hand support. Participants master the activity and then set a goal which upgrades their level of activity.

To become autonomous in the LiFE program participants learn how to upgrade their activities independently. The participant needs to understand the concept of upgrading activities and challenging themselves for when the therapist is no longer training them. Therapists also need to ensure that participants are able to perform activities and upgrade safely.

Finally, be sure to use positive reinforcement and encouragement. This can have a direct impact on therapist–client relationship and provides a safe and supportive environment for the client.

Gait

Understanding the connection between gait changes and falls risk may provide a motivation for older people to engage in balance and strength training to provide protection against falls.

The changes in gait in the older person may be influenced by a variety of factors including musculoskeletal changes such as decreased strength and range of motion at a variety of joints; neurological factors and confidence.

Gait analysis is extremely complex. However, a simplified analysis of the gait of older people generally states that older people have a shorter stride length, a wider base of support and a slower pace (Whittle 1991; Lord, Sherrington, & Menz, 2001). Anecdotally, many older people shuffle. This means that their feet are in contact with the ground for longer periods of time through the phases of the gait cycle. This may make them feel more stable, but may not necessarily protect them from falls. The inability to lift the foot to effectively clear an obstacle may make the person more likely to trip and therefore fall.

Improving balance and strength in the legs should translate to an improved ability to walk. For example, if the plantarflexors are strengthened the ability to push off the toe should be stronger; if the dorsiflexors are strengthened the ability to lift the forefoot should be improved, making the 'heel down' movement easier. Improving the strength and balance of the participant – including their ability to stand on one leg – provides a more stable supporting leg in the stance phase of the gait cycle. All these improvements should lead to an improvement in gait and therefore in the ability to walk confidently.

We encourage participants to think about the way they walk. They are encouraged to walk with 'heel down and toe off'. That is, they need to concentrate on making contact with their heel and then consciously pushing off with their toe. With improvements in both strength and balance the person should be encouraged to walk with an improved gait. They should also be encouraged to scan ahead as they walk (Clemson & Swann, 2008). The *Stepping on: building confidence and reducing falls, a community-based program for older people* (Clemson & Swann, 2008) has many useful strategies for safe mobility and confidence building when walking outdoors.

LiFE

Assessing ability and opportunity

Assessing ability and opportunity

Before teaching the program to participants therapists need to assess:

- opportunities in the participant's routine where LiFE activities can be embedded. This is done using the Daily Routine Chart (DRC).
- the ability of the participant in activities specifically related to the LiFE program. This is done using the LiFE Assessment Tool (LAT).

The assessments can also provide teaching opportunities. The LAT closely corresponds to the LiFE activities. As participants are being assessed you will be introducing some of the ideas on LiFE activities to them though not in a structured format.

The Daily Routine Chart (DRC)

The purpose of the Daily Routine Chart is to help identify opportunities in the daily routine of the participant where the LiFE balance and strength activities may be embedded.

Participants fill out the table outlining what they do each day for every day of the week. The more information participants can include in this form, the better able the therapist and participant will be to identify situations, places and times where the LiFE activities can be embedded.

The more detail that participants put in the chart the easier it is to determine opportunities to embed the activities. Routines or tasks that participants do on a weekly basis should be included. This could include involvement in community groups or activities, minding grandchildren, hobbies, regular outings, meetings or regular household task like taking out the garbage bins.

The DRC provides clues about where therapists can initially suggest LiFE activities may be included in their day. For example, the hallway between the bedrooms and the living area may be a good place to do the tandem walk, the kitchen sink may be a good place to do a tandem stand, or at the sink doing the washing up could be an opportunity to do a one-leg stand.

The DRC should be forwarded to the participant prior to their first session. At the first session the therapist will review the chart and may need to add more information to it. Some will require assistance to complete the form.

The amount of time that this will take to complete will depend on how well the participant fills the form in. Allow about 15 minutes to review this form if completed prior to session 1.

> **The LiFE Daily Routine Chart can be found on the following page. It can also be downloaded from the Sydney University Press website at purl.library.usyd.edu.au/sup/9781743320372.**

Life Daily Routine Chart (DRC)

List the activities that you do regularly on a daily and weekly basis

	Monday	Tuesday	Wednesday	Thursday	Friday	Saturday	Sunday
Morning	Get up	Get up	Get up	Get up	Get up	Get up	Get up
Afternoon	Lunch	Lunch	Lunch	Lunch	Lunch	Lunch	Lunch
Evening	Dinner	Dinner	Dinner	Dinner	Dinner	Dinner	Dinner
	Go to bed	Go to bed	Go to bed	Go to bed	Go to bed	Go to bed	Go to bed

The LiFE Assessment Tool (LAT)

The LiFE Assessment Tool (LAT) was designed specifically for the LiFE program. Trainers go through the LAT with the participant prior to starting the LiFE program to indicate at which level the participant should begin. The purpose of the tool is to provide an indication of the participant's ability to perform the LiFE activities. The assessments of balance and strength in the LAT are closely aligned to the activities in the LiFE program. The LAT also establishes a baseline for reassessment. If desired, the LiFE principles of balance and strength can be introduced to the participant while the therapist is performing the assessment.

Development of the LiFE Assessment Tool (LAT)

The LiFE Assessment Tool (LAT) was specifically designed to assess for the activities to be performed in the LiFE program. Initially, the LAT was a 19-item assessment that was developed for the pilot program. The tool was refined and validated with a sample of 80 people who participated in the randomised trial. The data was analysed and the tool validated by Laura Friery (Friery, 2007) as part of her occupational therapy undergraduate honours thesis. Results were analysed using Rasch modelling to explore item functioning and determine construct validity. After Rasch analysis it was modified to a briefer tool including those items that were most useful in showing different levels of ability and therefore warranted inclusion in the final tool. Some levels from a larger tool were collapsed and the final assessment was shown to be unidimensional with all items fitting one construct: dynamic balance. The refined 10-item scale is valid as an intervention planner and outcome measure.

What does the LiFE Assessment Tool consist of?

Musculoskeletal history

A short set of questions related to the lower limbs. All the questions should be answered and specific details recorded as appropriate. These may indicate any areas that may require precautions when implementing the LiFE activities.

Functional balance questions

A set of questions related to the performance of general ADL tasks that require balance.

LiFE balance and strength assessments

There are five balance activities and five strength activities to be assessed. The therapist should demonstrate each activity to the participant.

The balance and strength assessment is structured in the following manner:

- Column 1: describes the activity to be assessed. It also includes, where appropriate, the balance or strength principle related to that particular activity.
- Column 2, Instructions: gives brief instructions for the performance of the activity
- Columns 3–7, Levels 0–4: record the level at which the subject can perform the activity.
- Column 8, Notes: is to record any notes. This may include where the activity was performed or for how long it was performed.

Grading the levels for the balance and strength assessment

Each activity has been divided into levels related to the difficulty of the performance of the activity. The levels are graded from 0–4. However, not all activities have five levels of difficulty.

Subjects are assessed on each item at the highest level of difficulty they are able to safely achieve. It is not necessary to start the assessment at the lowest level. The assessor should use their judgment to select the ability level at which to begin testing. If the subject can safely perform at a certain level they should then attempt to perform the activity at the next level. The assessment of the activity should continue until they reach the highest level or are unable to perform the task. This should be done for all the activities listed. A system of ticks, circles and crosses is used to record the subject's ability (see examples below).

This information is used to determine at what level a participant should start with an activity. They will start at the highest level they can safely do.

Some items contain two tasks at the same level. The subject only needs to complete one of the tasks described in order to be recorded for that level. The choice of the task should be made in consultation with the subject. If the subject is unable to perform one of the tasks and there are no safety concerns they may attempt the alternative task.

The assessment does not need to be performed in the order that it is presented. There is no hierarchical structure to the assessment.

To implement the tool you will need the following:

- an A4 size piece of paper or coloured mat of A4 size
- foam block (approximately A4 size: 210 x 297 cm or 8.3 x 11.7 inches)
- stopwatch
- pens / pencils.

In one of the items the subject is required to add a mental distractor to the activity. The choice of distractor is up to the assessor and the subject. The most commonly used distractors are:

- to count backwards from 100 by 3s
- name a set of countries alphabetically
- names and dates of the birthdays of grandchildren.

The assessor should record which distractor was used.

You should allow 30 to 40 minutes to complete the assessment tool. However, this will vary depending on the ability of the participant. Allowances may need to be made for health and concentration levels. Participants are allowed to rest at any time during the assessment if needed.

> **The LiFE Assessment Tool and examples of a completed LiFE Assessment Tool can be found on the following pages. It can also be downloaded from the Sydney University Press website at purl.library.usyd.edu.au/sup/9781743320372.**

 **Assessment Tool**

Balance and strength assessments

Name:
DOB:
Age:
Date:

Musculoskeletal history

Do you have any arthritis in your knees or hips
Yes / No
Details:
If yes, which knee / hip has arthritis?

Do you have any joint replacements in your knees or hips?
Yes / No
Details:
If yes, which ones do you have?

Do you get, or have you ever had bursitis or tendonitis in your leg or legs?
Yes / No
Details:

Do you get or have you ever had low back pain?
Yes / No
Details:

Functional balance questions

Do you sit or stand when dressing? If both, do you mostly sit or mostly stand?
Sit / Mostly sit / Mostly stand / Stand

Do you sit down or stand up to put on your shoes and socks?
Sit / Stand

Do you sit down or stand up to put on your pants?
Sit / Stand

Do you sit down or stand up to put on your bra / singlet?
Sit / Stand

Do you sit down or stand up to shower? If bath, do you sit in bottom of bath?
Sit in shower / Stand in shower / Stand up in bath / Sit down in bath

During your shower do you hold onto anything for support?
Yes / No

How confident are you that you can get dressed without losing your balance?
Not at all confident / A little confident / Fairly confident / Very confident

Do you use a walking stick or walking frame?
Yes / No

If yes, when do you use it?
Always / When going out / Varies – I use it as needed

Are you able to step down a curb or gutter without assistance?
Yes / No

LiFE Assessment Tool: balance activities

Decreased base of support	Instructions	Level 0	Level 1	Level 2	Level 3	Level 4	Notes
1. Tandem stand	Heel-to-toe stand. Support available. Weight transferred in a forwards / backwards direction.	Tandem stand with constant support. OR Unable to perform.	Tandem stand with intermittent support.	Tandem stand with no support.	Tandem stand with no support while brushing hair OR with eyes shut.		
2. Tandem walk	Have support available. Distance walked should be approximately 1.5 metres.	Tandem walk with constant support. OR Unable to perform.	Tandem walk with intermittent support.	Tandem walk with no support.	Tandem walk with no support with eyes shut.		Record where activity is done:
3. One-leg stand	Record the leg that is least stable.	Single-leg stand with constant support. Least stable leg: Left / Right OR Unable to perform.	Single-leg stand with intermittent support. Least stable leg: Left / Right	Single-leg stand with no support. Least stable leg: Left / Right	Single-leg stand with no support while doing something else such as getting object from cupboard at shoulder height. Least stable leg: Left / Right	Single-leg stand with no support with eyes shut. Least stable leg: Left / Right	

Shifting weight and moving to the limits of stability	Instructions	Level 0	Level 1	Level 2	Level 3	Level 4	Notes
4. Leaning forwards and backwards	Stand on both feet. Lean as far as possible forward, shifting the weight onto the toes. Do not bend at the waist or neck. Aim to hold for 10 seconds.	Stand with feet shoulder-width apart; use constant support. Hold for 10 seconds. OR Unable to perform.	Stand with feet shoulder-width apart; use no support. Time position held:	Stand with feet together; use no support. Hold for 10 seconds.	Stand with feet together; use no support. Hold for 10 seconds while using a mental distractor OR hold for 10 seconds with eyes closed.		Record which mental distractor was used:
Stepping over objects	**Instructions**	**Level 0**	**Level 1**	**Level 2**	**Level 3**	**Level 4**	**Notes**
5. Forwards and backwards	Place an A4-size marker on the floor. The subject should step forward and then backwards over the marker. Ensure that support is available, e.g. the door frame.	Step in both directions using a support. OR Unable to perform.	Step in both directions without using support.	Step over foam block without using support.	Step over foam block without using support while doing another task such as carrying a dinner plate OR with eyes shut.		

LiFE Assessment Tool: strength activities

Bend the knees	Instructions	Level 0	Level 1	Level 2	Level 3	Level 4	Notes
6. Squatting	Have support available. The exercise should be pain free. Do not aim for a full squat.	Partial squat with support. OR Unable to perform.	Partial squat with no support. Hold for five seconds.	Half squat with no support. Hold for five seconds. OR Get something from below the sink using a squat.			

On your toes	Instructions	Level 0	Level 1	Level 2	Level 3	Level 4	Notes
7. Walking on toes	Heels must be off the ground for entire distance walked. Distance should be approximately 1.5 metres.	Unable to perform Level 1.	Walk on toes using constant support.	Walk on toes using intermittent or no support.	Walk on toes using no support while doing something else such as carrying a plate with a biscuit on it.	Walk on toes using no support with eyes shut.	Record where activity done:

On your heels	Instructions	Level 0	Level 1	Level 2	Level 3	Level 4	Notes
8. Walking on heels	Toes must be off the ground for entire distance walked. Distance should be approximately 1.5 metres.	Unable to perform Level 1.	Walk on heels using constant support.	Walk on heels using intermittent support.	Walk on heels using no support while doing something else such as carrying. a plate with a biscuit on it.	Walk on heels using no support with eyes shut.	Record where activity done:

Sit to stand / stand to sit	Instructions	Level 0	Level 1	Level 2	Level 3	Level 4	Notes
9. Standing up from a seated position	Assessor demonstrates correct technique: Sit with bottom to front of chair. Lean forward. Push up from legs. Avoid rocking. Use hand support as required.	Rising from standard chair with hand support. OR Unable to perform.	Rising from standard chair No hand support.	Rising from a low chair With hand support	Rising from a low chair slowly. No hand support Must take at least 5 seconds		Record the chair used in the assessment:
Move sideways	**Instructions**	**Level 0**	**Level 1**	**Level 2**	**Level 3**	**Level 4**	**Notes**
10. Move sideways.	Walk by stepping sideways. Support should be available. Subjects should aim to take the widest step they can safely perform. Assessor may need to demonstrate.	Sideways walk with steps that are shoulder-width or less apart, using support. OR Unable to perform.	Sideways walk with steps that are wider than shoulder-width apart, using support.	Sideways walk with steps that are wider than shoulder-width apart, using no support.			If support is required, record where activity was assessed:

Examples of how to fill out the LAT

In Table 1 the assessor started at level 1 and the subject was able to perform at that level. The assessor would then ask the subject to attempt level 2.

Table 1

Decreased base of support	Instructions	Level 0	Level 1	Level 2	Level 3	Level 4	Notes
1. Tandem stand	Heel-to-toe stand. Support available. Weight transferred in a forwards / backwards direction.	Tandem stand with constant support. OR Unable to perform.	Tandem stand with intermittent support. ✓	Tandem stand with no support.	Tandem stand with no support while brushing hair OR with eyes shut.		

Table 2 shows a subject who could perform the task at level 1 and 2 however was unable to perform the task at level 3.

Table 3.

Decreased base of support	Instructions	Level 0	Level 1	Level 2	Level 3	Level 4	Notes
1. Tandem stand	Heel-to-toe stand. Support available. Weight transferred in a forwards / backwards direction.	Tandem stand with constant support. OR Unable to perform.	Tandem stand with intermittent support. ✓	Tandem stand with no support. ✓	Tandem stand with no support while brushing hair OR with eyes shut. ✗		

Table 3 demonstrates a situation where the assessor began the assessment at level 1 and the participant was unable to perform the activity. The assessor asked the subject to perform the task at level 0 and the subject was able to perform the activity in the manner that was circled. Table 4 is the same situation as Table 3. However, the subject was not able to perform the activity as is indicated by the circle.

Table 3

Decreased base of support	Instructions	Level 0	Level 1	Level 2	Level 3	Level 4	Notes
1. Tandem stand	Heel-to-toe stand. Support available. Weight transferred in a forwards / backwards direction.	(circled) Tandem stand with constant support. OR Unable to perform.	Tandem stand with intermittent support. ✗	Tandem stand with no support.	Tandem stand with no support while brushing hair OR with eyes shut.		

Table 4

Decreased base of support	Instructions	Level 0	Level 1	Level 2	Level 3	Level 4	Notes
1. Tandem stand	Heel-to-toe stand. Support available. Weight transferred in a forwards / backwards direction.	Tandem stand with constant support. ✗ OR (circled) Unable to perform.	Tandem stand with intermittent support.	Tandem stand with no support. ✗	Tandem stand with no support while brushing hair OR with eyes shut.		

Table 5 shows a similar situation to Tables 3 and 4. However, for this item Level 0 contains only an unable to perform rating.

Table 5

On your toes	Instructions	Level 0	Level 1	Level 2	Level 3	Level 4	Notes
7. Walking on toes	Heels must be off the ground for entire distance walked. Distance should be approximately 1.5 metres.	Unable to perform Level 1	Walk on toes using constant support.	Walk on toes using intermittent or no support.	Walk on toes using no support while doing something else such as carrying a plate with a biscuit on it.	Walk on toes using no support with eyes shut.	Record where activity done:

Table 6 shows that the subject was not able to perform the first element of level 2 but was able to perform the second element in the level.

Table 6

Bend the knees	Instructions	Level 0	Level 1	Level 2	Level 3	Level 4	Notes
6. Squatting	Have support available. The exercise should be pain free. Do not aim for a full squat.	Partial squat with support. OR Unable to perform.	Partial squat with no support. Hold for five seconds.	Half squat with no support. Hold for five seconds. OR Get something from below the sink using a squat.			

Other assessments

There are a number of other assessment tools that can be used to assess falls risk and mobility (e.g. timed get-up-and-go, timed tandem walk, static balance assessments) and those that can be used as baseline measures to assess outcomes. The choice to use assessments other than those listed above has not been factored into the timeframes listed in the implementation of the program.

LiFE

Teaching the program

Teaching the program

Trainers must have read the participant's manual before reading the following section. The participant's manual has pictures and diagrams which will enhance the understanding of the following section. You should refer to it as you work through this information.

> **It is important to teach participants the principles not just the activities. As you are explaining the principles, demonstrate what the principle is and give examples of how it applies to improving function or gait, or to preventing falls. You should also demonstrate the activities as you teach them.**

Teaching the program

Initial stages

The structure for teaching the participant the LiFE program should be carried out in the following manner:

- Teach the balance and strength principles, including functional examples and relevance to improving function, gait and preventing falls.

- Teach the participant the chosen activity and reinforce the principle related to it.

- Demonstrate the activity to the participant. Refer to the Daily Routine Chart to determine where the participant might plan to embed specific activities.

- Have the participant perform the activity in the situation that they are likely to perform the activity. When this is not possible, help them visualise practicing it in the situation (for example, at the supermarket).

- Correct the participant's technique as necessary.

- Encourage the participant to visualise how, when and where the activities will be done.

- Have the participant plan where they are going to perform the activity. This includes the location and daily task that it will be connected with.

- Have the participant practice the activity. While they are practicing explain to them the benefits of doing that particular exercise.

- Show the participant the relevant section of the participant's manual.

- Reinforce key points and tips.

- Check and reinforce any precautions to ensure the activity is being performed safely.
- Ensure the plan for the activity performance is recorded on the Activity Planner.

Each time you are teaching or introducing a new activity you will need to go through the above steps.

Progressing through LiFE

Participants will need multiple sessions to learn the program. Some will grasp the concepts quickly and completely; others will take much longer. The above steps can be used for teaching until all the activities have been introduced.

After the initial session:

- Encourage the participant to perform the activity in different parts of the house or embed the activity in different daily tasks.

- Encourage the participant to come up with ideas for where the activities could be embedded into their daily routine. This increases the autonomy of the participant in the LiFE program. It shifts the focus from the therapist being prescriptive to participants being independent.

- Ask the participant to complete the Activity Planner and the Activity Counter. Completing these forms is critical to reinforcing the activities (see section on 'Planning and recording performance of the LiFE activities').

- Demonstrate how and encourage them to upgrade activities to ensure that they are able to continue to challenge themselves.

The above teaching strategies can be introduced as early as the first session. However, this will depend on the participant's ability to understand the principles and carry out the activities.

A few additional points on teaching the program

Linking activities to situational cues and prompts

Encourage participants to connect or link the activities to specific daily tasks or routines. For example, if they choose to perform a tandem stand while they are brushing their teeth, the task of teeth-brushing becomes the cue or prompt to do the tandem stand. This is an example of how the LiFE activity is embedded in the daily routine.

Changing the environment

Participants should also be encouraged to change their environment to facilitate increasing the opportunities to embed the activities. This might include moving everyday items to different positions in the house to prompt the performance of specific activities. For example, the participant could move the toothpaste to a lower shelf so that they are prompted to perform a knee bend to reach it, or they could move coffee cups to a slightly higher shelf so that they are prompted to stand on their toes when they reach for the cups.

Look for opportunities to upgrade

Upgrading can be challenging for many people. Some people like to have a set activity to perform. The therapist facilitates the concept that participants should continuously upgrade their activities and challenge themselves.

For example, the participant could perform the LiFE activities alongside a kitchen bench using intermittent hand support. The kind of support depends on the activity and the participant's level of capacity. They should be encouraged to decrease their hand support as their balance improves.

Trainers continuously refer the participants to the participant's manual for instructions, photographs and helpful tips on the activities. This is their workbook and they need to keep it, use it and write in if they wish.

Teaching the balance training principles and activities

Trainers should refer to the participant's manual for instructions, photographs and tips for the activities.

Key points

To improve their balance, participants have to practice a challenging balance activity. For their balance to continue to improve they need to keep upgrading to a more challenging balance activity or level.

Always demonstrate the activity to the participant. If possible, do this in the situation you think they might do it in.

The principles of LiFE balance training

- reducing your base of support
- shifting weight and moving to the limits of stability
- stepping over objects.

Reducing your base of support

Explanation and demonstration of principle

Your base of support is all the parts of you that are in contact with the floor or something that is holding you up. You increase your base of support when you use your hands to support yourself or you use a walking stick. As you reduce your base of support you increase the difficulty of balancing. It is more challenging for your balance to stand or move with a narrow base of support.

A wide base of support can be shown by standing with feet apart holding onto a chair or table. Demonstrate how bringing the feet together and not using hand support decreases the base of support and increases the balance challenge.

Relevance to everyday function

It is not often that anyone would need to perform tandem standing or walking in everyday life, but there are some situations where you do need to be able to stand on one leg, such as to put on your shoes, socks and pants or to dry your feet after a shower. Practicing tandem standing or walking is an effective way of improving balance and improving the participant's ability to function in daily tasks. During the gait cycle there are phases where you are standing on one leg as you swing the opposite leg through. By practicing standing on one leg you have the potential to improve your walking or gait as well as protect you from falling.

The focus on decreasing the base of support must always be considered in the context of safety.

LiFE activities that involve a reduced base of support:

1. tandem stand
2. tandem walk
3. one-leg stand.

Instructions for teaching activities related to the principle of reducing your base of support

1. Tandem stand

This is best performed where the participant has access to stable support. This could include (but is not limited to) kitchen or bathroom benches, dining tables or stable chairs. You should perform a tandem stand by having the toes of one foot in line with the heel of the other foot.

You should show the participant how to perform the activity starting with hand support. Then show them how to decrease hand support by removing one hand, then by using only finger tips for support, then removing all hand support. An easy upgrade for tandem stand is to shift weight backwards and forwards, and this can also be done while performing a daily task such as washing up.

2. Tandem walk

This is safest to demonstrate where there is stable support such as a kitchen bench or dining table, that is, a support at least one to two metres in length. Hallways are also good as participants can use the walls for support.

> **Participants need to understand that correct performance with hand support is more desirable than speed and poor performance.**

3. One-leg stand

Demonstrate this in a similar manner to the tandem stand. Standing on one leg is the smallest base of support.

Help the participant understand that the amount of support may vary each time they do the activity. This is because some days we need a little more support than other days and also the activity may be more challenging in different situations.

Shifting weight and moving to the limits of stability

Explanation and demonstration of principle

For good balance you need to be able to maintain your stability when you shift your weight as you move. When you lean to one side (keeping your spine straight) you are shifting your body weight to just short of where you lose your balance and we call this moving to the limits of stability. If you can smoothly and safely shift your weight in either a sideways or forwards and backwards direction then you will be less likely to lose your balance.

Demonstrate by leaning and reaching so that you are moving to the limit of stability.

Shifting your weight from foot to foot becomes more difficult as you decrease your base of support. You can make moving to the limits of stability more difficult by decreasing your base of support or by holding at the limit for a longer time.

Relevance to daily function

When you reach to get something that is just beyond your reach you shift your weight in one direction and move to the limits of stability. For example, you shift your weight backwards when you are washing your hair with both hands while standing, or when drawing the curtains. Walking up and down ramps requires you to shift your weight forwards going up and shift your weight back as you go down to maintain your balance.

LiFE activities that involve shifting weight and moving to the limits of stability:

1. leaning from side to side
2. leaning forwards and backwards.

Instructions for teaching activities related to the principle of shifting weight and moving to the limits of stability

1. Leaning from side to side

Stand with feet shoulder-width apart, shift weight onto the right foot keeping the left foot on the ground, and lean as far as possible to the right; hold this position. Repeat the movement, moving to the opposite side. Make sure you do not bend at the waist, that is, keep your back in a straight line.

2. Leaning forwards and backwards

Stand with feet shoulder-width apart, shift weight forwards feeling the weight through the toes but keeping heels on the ground. Then shift weight backwards onto the heels, feeling the weight through the heels but keeping the toes on the ground. Make sure not to bend at the waist.

For both the above activities participants should have support readily available.

This activity can be made more challenging in a number of ways. The participant can:

- bring their feet closer together
- hold for longer at the end of the movement
- decrease the amount of support that they use from their hands.

An advanced activity is performing the leaning forwards and backwards movement in a tandem stand. This is a combination of principles and activities and is an upgrade of both activities. There are many opportunities to upgrade as participants improve.

Stepping over objects

Explanation and demonstration of principle

Being able to safely and confidently step over objects is important in situations where we need to deal with obstacles like gutters and uneven surfaces. You need to be able to step forwards and backwards as well as side to side. The high step takes longer than a normal step and makes your supporting leg work harder to balance. You should demonstrate with support available. A doorway can be a good place to start. You should step up and over using a high stepping motion. The following leg should also be moved in a high stepping motion.

Relevance to everyday function

You may need to step over or around an extension cord, a child's toy, a spill on the supermarket floor or an uneven footpath. We may be aware of the lead foot and clearing the obstacle but the following foot may catch on the object and disturb our balance. For this reason it is important to practice concentrating on the performance of both feet.

LiFE Activities that involve stepping over objects:

1. stepping over objects: forwards and backwards
2. stepping over objects: side to side.

Instructions for teaching activities related to the principle of stepping over objects

1. Stepping over objects: forwards and backwards

Place a piece of paper or cloth on the floor. Step over the object in an exaggerated manner. You should lift your leading foot high, up and over. The following foot also needs to be lifted in an 'up and over' manner. The foot that follows is just as important as the leading foot. Participants should step one foot forward and follow with the other foot. They should then step backwards with one foot and follow with the other. Participants should alternate the foot that they use to lead the step.

2. Stepping over objects: side to side

Stepping over objects in a side-to-side movement performed the same way as the forwards-and-backwards movement except that it is done sideways.

For both the above activities support should be readily available. Participants are encouraged to start with support, but to gradually decrease this as they are more confident in stepping forwards and backwards and side to side.

Teaching order for balance activities

There is no set order in which these must be taught. Most participants find the activities for reduced base of support the easiest to start with. The tandem stand and one-leg stand are not necessarily the easiest activities to perform but participants seem to find the concept easy to grasp. These are usually relatively easy to embed into daily activities.

Therapists can decide with individual participants how they would like to incorporate the challenge upgrades as it may depend on what daily task the participant is embedding the activity in.

More ways to challenge balance

To improve balance you have to continually challenge balance. When performing the balance activities in this manual, participants can challenge their balance further in the following ways:

Reduce the amount of support from the hands

This can be done gradually in the following way:

- hold with two hands
- hold with one hand
- hold with finger tips, two fingers tips, one finger tip
- intermittent support – use support on and off or for part of the time
- no hand support.

Combine the balance principles

By combining the balance principles the participant can also challenge their balance.

For example, the participant can combine the principles of reducing your base of support and shifting weight and moving to the limits of stability.

When the participant is able to shift their weight from foot to foot easily with their feet wide apart, they can make it more difficult by reducing their base of support by bringing their feet closer together.

Advanced activities to further challenge balance

As participants gain confidence they may want to further challenge their balance ability. The following activities can be added to any of the balance activities. It is important that participants understand how to challenge their balance but that they understand how to do this safely.

Closing your eyes

Closing your eyes makes it harder to balance because we usually rely on sight to help us balance. However, there are occasions when we do need to do things without sight or vision. By practicing balancing with the eyes closed it is helpful for situations where the participant may find themselves in a darkened room or on a poorly lit street.

Doing something else at the same time

By doing something else while trying to balance the participant is challenging their balance even further as the brain is trying to do more than one thing at the same time. Functional examples of this include talking to someone, carrying something or performing a daily task while balancing.

Doing a mentally demanding activity at the same time

Doing a mentally demanding activity is another way to challenge balance. Again the brain has to think of more than one thing at the same time. If you want to do a task like tandem walking and make it more challenging you can try naming your grandchildren's birthdays, or listing as many animals as you can alphabetically.

Upgrading balance activities

Upgrading is a key component of the program. It is important for participants to upgrade the balance activities that they are performing. Therapists will need to instruct participants on how to safely upgrade their activities.

The decision to incorporate additional balance challenges will depend on the participant's ability. When helping participants to work out how to upgrade their activities a general rule is to try to get them to reduce the amount of support they use from their hands first. This is a very easy concept for most people to grasp. It also means that their hands are then free to be involved in their normal tasks. They should be encouraged to follow the strategy for decreasing support from their hands outlined above.

Although we use the very ordered LAT to assess participants, participants can practice balance activities in any order. Challenging balance does not have to be a hierarchical structure. For example, some participants may still want support from one hand or fingertips but like to close their eyes. Some will find that they want to add a little support as they try a more challenging activity. However, we would strongly recommend that they only add one challenge at a time. For example, a participant should not go from holding on with two hands to fingertip support *and* do something else at the same time. Rather they should decrease their hand support *or* do something else at the same time. Participants should try to perform a balance activity well before adding any additional challenge. This relates back to the idea of mastery of activities.

Overall, the program focuses on trying to encourage participants to challenge their balance while ensuring their safety at the same time.

> **How many do I have to do?**
>
> **Participants are not required to perform a specific number of any of the activities. The focus is instead on doing as many as the participant can and always finding ways of doing more.**

Teaching the strength training principles and activities

Trainers should refer to the participant's manual for instructions, photographs and tips on the activities.

Key points

To improve muscle strength you need to load the muscles. This means making the muscles work harder. When doing the LiFE strength training activities, participants need look for ways to load their muscles.

Muscles groups that will protect the participant from falls are listed in the participant's manual. They are the muscles in the legs. As part of the LiFE activity program participants need to learn how to include the principles underlying strength training and the strength activities into their daily routine to improve the strength of the leg muscles.

The principles of LiFE strength training

You can load your muscles in a number of ways. You can:

- increase the number of times that you use a muscle
- move slowly – this can make the muscles work harder
- use fewer muscles to move the same weight
- increase the amount of weight you have to lift or move.

The explanation and demonstration of strength principle is done slightly differently to how it was done for balance. With all the strength activities you can use the principle of loading muscles. Participants need to understand that they need to load their muscles by doing the activities and then work on the above methods to increase the load on their muscles.

LiFE activities that involve loading your muscles:

1. **bend your knees**
2. **sit to stand**
3. **on your toes: standing and walking**
4. **on your heels: standing and walking**
5. **up the stairs**
6. **walk sideways**
7. **tighten muscles.**

1. Bend your knees

Explanation

Partial and full squatting is an easy and effective way to improve and maintain knee and quadriceps strength. Many people are scared of squats because of arthritis in their knees. This is why we have not used the term 'squat' but rather the phrase 'bend your knees'. It doesn't need to be a full squat. Any level of knee bend will help to improve the strength of the muscles around the knees. If there are problems with arthritis in the knee joints, ensure that the knee bends are in the pain-free range of movement.

Relevance to everyday function

Strong quadriceps muscles improve knee stability and improve the functional ability to go up stairs and get out of chairs. Practising squats and partial squats is an effective way to strengthen the quadriceps.

Demonstration

Pick something up from a coffee table or low shelf by bending your knees instead of bending at the hips or back.

Every time the participant does something below waist height they should try to bend their knees. In everyday life there are numerous occasions when the participant can bend their knees instead of their back.

2. Sit to stand

Explanation

Older people will often push themselves up from a chair relying heavily on their arms. By using good technique to get out of a chair they can rely more on their legs and at the same time strengthen their legs.

Relevance to everyday function

Being able to stand up from a chair confidently enables participants to be comfortable in a variety of situations. Many social settings have chairs that do not have any arms. By practicing getting out of a chair without using their arms, the participant will find that they improve their confidence in getting out of a variety of chairs.

Demonstration

The following explanation refers to 'normal chairs' and 'low chairs'. A 'normal' chair is a dining room or kitchen chair or similar. A 'low' chair is a lounge chair or sofa. It is more difficult to stand up from sitting in a low chair because it requires the person to lift their body further and the person has less mechanical advantage to assist them to stand.

Show the participant how many people rely on using chair arms or a table in front of them to push themselves out of a chair. Demonstrate how to move to the front of the chair, lean the body forwards over the thighs and then use the legs to push up. It is ok for the participant to use their arms initially but they should understand how to decrease the use of their arms to improve the strength in their legs.

Although the low chair is more challenging participants can practice using this type of chair provided it is safe for them to do so. This would be determined using the LAT.

3. On your toes: standing and walking

Explanation

Standing or walking on your toes will help to strengthen the plantarflexors (calf muscles).

Relevance to everyday function

Strong plantarflexors are important as they help to push the foot off from the ground, propelling the body forward and enabling the person to stride out.

Demonstration: standing

Reach for something above shoulder height and stand on your toes as you do this. Although you may be tall enough not to need to stand on your toes to reach for something above shoulder height the idea is that the reaching becomes the prompt for you to go on your toes and therefore strengthen your calf muscles.

For example, the participant could stand on their toes when reaching up to get something out of the kitchen cupboard, off a high shelf in the laundry or when getting clothes out of the wardrobe. The shelf or cupboard doesn't need to be high – anything above waist height can be the prompt for the 'on your toes' activity.

It is ok if the participant needs to support themselves at first with one hand while the other is reaching, but they will gradually be able to decrease the amount of hand support needed.

Demonstration: walking

The participant should always start with support available. The kitchen bench, dining room table or the hallway are good places to start. The participant should walk on their toes, keeping their heels off the ground. Many participants can only lift their heels a small way off the floor.

4. On your heels: standing and walking

Explanation

Standing or walking on your heels helps to strengthen the dorsiflexors (the muscles at the front of the calf). It is also a challenging balance activity.

Relevance to everyday function

These muscles are important as they are responsible for lifting the forefoot up, helping it to clear the ground when walking and stepping.

Demonstration: standing

Go back onto your heels while standing at the kitchen or bathroom bench. Initially demonstrate this movement while holding onto something, as this is a particularly difficult activity.

Demonstration: walking

Always start this activity with support. Walk along the kitchen bench or hallway on your heels, trying to keep the toes off the floor. Explain that it is often easier to walk on your heels than it is to stand on your heels. At first the participant may need to support themselves with their hands, but as their muscles get stronger and their balance improves it will get easier to stand or walk on their heels and they can gradually decrease the amount of support needed. Participants will still improve their strength even if they need to continue to use support

As well as being good strengthening activities, the 'on your toes' and 'on your heels' activities are good balance activities.

5. Up the stairs

Explanation

Going up stairs is an extremely good exercise to strengthen the knee muscles.

Relevance to everyday function

Often people will limit where they go if they are unable to or lack the confidence to climb up stairs. Having the ability to negotiate stairs confidently improves a person's ability to remain independent in the community.

Demonstration

Many people walk up stairs using the banister or rail to pull themselves up. Show how using your legs to push up off the stair and onto the next one will help to strengthen them. If participants are nervous about letting the handrail go, show them how they can gradually decrease the amount of support needed from the railing.

Many people actively limit the amount of times they use the stairs. Explain that each time they go up the stairs they are strengthening their leg muscles.

The activity is practised only going *up* the stairs, never down the stairs, for safety reasons. The stairs chosen for practice should have a handrail and be free from clutter. Remind enthusiastic participants not to overdo the stairs activity. Instead, they should start slowly and build up the number of times participants include the stairs.

An advanced activity for this is to go up the stairs two at a time.

6. Walk sideways

Explanation

The hip abductors are an important group of muscles as they stabilise the hip on the support leg when walking. Weak hip abductors are sometimes the cause of falls. Walking or stepping sideways helps to strengthen the hip abductors. This is not a movement we do very often in everyday life so LiFE encourages increasing these opportunities.

Relevance to everyday function

Most of the time we walk in a forward or backward direction however there are times when we may have to walk or step sideways, for example, when manoeuvring around tables and chairs, walking into a crowded lift or walking along a narrow path. Stepping sideways with strength and good balance can prevent a fall when moving in this way.

Demonstration

Have support available, for example, the kitchen bench or dining table. Demonstrate how to walk in a sideways direction by abducting the leg and swinging it to the side then adducting the opposite leg to meet it. Demonstrate the movement in both directions.

7. Tighten muscles

By tightening the muscles that are resting, such as the ankles, knees and buttocks, you can increase the load on them and strengthen them.

This is more like 'traditional' exercises. For the ankles exercise, participants should move their ankles up and down (this exercises the dorsiflexors and plantarflexors). To strengthen the knees, participants should straighten their knee and hold it in position for a few seconds. To exercise the buttocks, participants should squeeze their buttocks, hold for a few seconds, then release. Participants can do this whenever they are sitting for extended periods of time. This could be during the ads while watching TV, waiting for the bus or train, or waiting at the doctor or hairdresser.

Teaching order for strength activities

There is no set order for teaching the strength activities or hierarchy to the implementation. Most people find 'bend the knees', 'sit to stand' and 'up the stairs' the easiest activities to grasp. Although the activities to tighten muscles are conceptually more simple, some people struggle to remember it. Use caution if commencing knee bends and the up the stairs activities at the same time as both of these activities have the potential to irritate knees with degenerative arthritis. Therapists should help participants choose activities that are initially easy to embed into their daily routine.

Upgrading

The strategies for loading muscles to increase strength will be implemented differently, depending on the participant. This is because the program is individually tailored to each participant. For example, when practising the 'sit to stand' activity, some participants will increase the number of times they include the activity; others will chose to perform the activity slowly; others will be capable of increasing the number and performing it slowly. Participants do not need to upgrade in any specific order. Furthermore, the way that participants load their muscles will depend on how they embed the activities into their routine. For most participants, increasing the number of times that they use a muscle or set of muscles is the simplest way to load their muscles.

> **How many do I have to do?**
>
> **As with the balance activities, participants are not required to perform a specific number of any of the strength activities. The best way to improve muscle strength is to do as many activities as you can and to always look for opportunities to do more.**

LiFE

A guide for what to do in each session

A guide for what to do in each session

The following section provides information about what you need to do in each session. As with all clinical interventions, professional judgement needs to be used to determine what each participant is capable of. For the majority of participants you will be able to implement the inclusion of the LiFE activities according to these guidelines. However, there will be others who will require a slower implementation and those who will be able to achieve more at a faster pace.

Session 1

The aim of session 1 is to assess the participant and to introduce them to the principles of the LiFE program and the balance and strength activities that the participant will embed in their daily routine.

The first session usually takes at least one and a half hours. In this first session the therapist needs to perform the following:

1. **Assess the participant's ability and daily routine.**
2. **Orientate the participant to the program and the manual.**
3. **Teach the key concepts and principles.**
4. **Teach the selected activities.**
5. **Plan and record how, when and where the activities will be performed.**
6. **Wrap up.**

1. Assess the participant's ability and daily routine

Assess the participant's daily routine for opportunities

The trainer is expected to use the **Daily Routine Chart (DRC)** to assess the participant's daily and weekly routine. This is to identify how the LiFE program may be implemented and the associated activities embedded into the participant's routine. See section on 'Assessing ability and opportunity' for a copy of the DRC, examples and instructions.

Assess the participant

The trainer is expected to use the **LiFE Assessment Tool (LAT)** to assess the capabilities of the participant. The LAT takes approximately thirty minutes to complete. However, allowances need to be made for health and concentration levels of the participant. For instructions on the administration of the LAT see section on 'Assessing ability and opportunity'.

2. Orientate the participant to the program and the manual

The therapist should have read the participant's manual thoroughly and be familiar with its layout. The therapist will need to go through the participant's manual with the participant and explain the format of the manual and the structure of the program. It is important to point out the key points, instructions, photographs of the activities and the tips on how to perform the activities correctly.

3. Teach the key concepts and principles

This is an overview of general topics that need to be covered in this first session. For detailed information about how to teach the activities, refer to the previous section of this trainer's manual.

Although concepts, principles and activities are written separately in this manual they are usually taught concurrently. For example, you might be explaining the principle to reduce the base of support. You might demonstrate a tandem stand and discuss how this activity could be incorporated into a daily routine by the participant performing the activity at the bathroom sink while brushing their teeth.

Key concepts

- Embedding activities into daily routine
- changing your habits
- looking for opportunities to perform the activities
- challenging yourself
- safety.

It is essential to understand these concepts to effectively teach the program. This information is covered in detail in this manual in the Background section. It is also covered in the participant's manual.

© Clemson, Munro and Fiatarone Singh 2014

Principles of balance training:

- reducing your base of support
- shifting weight and moving to the limits of stability
- stepping over objects.

Principles of strength training:

- increase the number of times that you use a muscle
- move slowly – this can make the muscles work harder
- use fewer muscles to move the same weight
- increase the amount of weight you have to lift or move.

4. Teach the selected activities

The number and choice of activities will depend on the individual participant, their daily routine and what you assess as being most easily embedded and integrated activities. The LAT and the DRC are used to help determine the most appropriate level to commence the activities in a manner that is challenging but safe. There is detailed information on this in the section on 'Teaching the program'. As you teach each activity, refer to the participant's manual to show the participant where the activity is in the manual.

Teach 1–2 balance activities

You can start with any of the balance activities. However, most participants find the activities for reduced base of support the easiest to start with. A suggestion would be to start with the tandem stand, one-leg stand, or tandem walk. These are not necessarily the easiest activities, but participants seem to find the concept and the activity easy to grasp.

Teach 1–2 strength activities

You can start with any of the strength activities. However, most participants find 'bend the knees' and 'sit to stand' activities reasonably easy to embed into their daily routine.

5. Plan and record how, when and where the activities will be performed

> **Trainers need to explain the importance of planning and recording these plans. It is central to the process of habit change and formation and reinforces achievements.**

Complete the Activity Planner

This will include the balance and strength activities that the participant is planning to practise over the next week and the daily tasks into which the participant intends to embed the activity. It also records what the participant does each day, which reinforces the performance of the activities.

The Activity Planner provides an opportunity for participants to visualise and plan their commitment. It includes recording how, when and where the participant will embed their strength and balance activities. This provides a prompt to the situation and the context. The Activity Planner is used to record what the participant does each day which reinforces the performance of the activities.

Complete the Activity Counter

This will include the balance activity and the strength activity that the participant will be counting over the next week. Usually participants count one balance and one strength activity for one day each week. The Activity Counter provides a snapshot of one or two selected LiFE activities to provide feedback and further reinforcement.

The Activity Planner and the Activity Counter together help to identify achievements and areas of difficulty that participants may be having.

For detailed information on recording see section on 'Planning and recording performance of the LiFE activities'.

6. Wrap up

Make it clear what the participant needs to do between sessions 1 and 2, which is to:

- read the manual
- do the activities taught in session 1
- fill in the activity planning sheets every day
- set a plan related to which balance and strength activity they will count and on which day they will count each of these
- count one to two activities on the days that they choose
- be aware of safety. In the early stages the participant should check with a therapist before upgrading their activities.

Encourage participants to think about what they would like to achieve. Both short-term and long-term goals are important. An example of a long-term goal may be to stay in the home they are currently in, to continue doing voluntary work, or to be able to go on holidays or to a family function. A short-term goal may be to do tandem walk down the hallway when they are going to the bedroom. This short-term goal is really an activity related goal.

> There is a lot of information to absorb and it is not expected that participants will understand everything at the first training session. It is a lifestyle change so it may take time for participants to grasp the concepts and activities.

Sessions 2–5

Throughout these sessions the participant should gradually increase their autonomy in managing the program. Trainers should facilitate the participants coming up with their own ideas of where activities might be embedded.

Each participant will be upgraded differently according to their starting levels and their progress. Implementation and upgrading is done in consultation with the participant. In the early stages it is prudent to have participants check with you before upgrading their activities. However, by the end of training they should be able to competently and safely upgrade their own activities.

Sessions 2–4 are done at weekly intervals.

Session 5 should be conducted after a break of at least one week. This allows the participant to have some autonomy in setting and adjusting the program. It also allows the therapist to review whether the participant is able to manage independently.

 The aim of sessions 2–5 is for the participant to become autonomous in applying the LiFE program. They should be able to independently integrate the LiFE activities into their daily routine and safely upgrade their activities.

Before session 2 the participant should have:

- familiarised themselves with the entire manual – its layout and contents
- done at least one balance and one strength activity in the previous week
- have filled in the activity recording sheets.

By the end of session 2 the participant should:

- be able to do between two to four additional balance and strength activities
- have begun to identify for themselves daily tasks where LiFE activities can be embedded.

By the end of session 5 the participant should be able to:

- perform at least 10 or all of the activities in the LiFE program
- complete the activity recording sheets (the Activity Planner and Activity Counter) correctly
- identify areas / activities where they will be able to embed LiFE activities into their daily routine
- manage to independently continue the program safely.

Each of the sessions (2–5) should take approximately one hour. At each of the sessions the therapist / trainer should complete the following:

1. **Review the balance and strength activities commenced previously.**

2. **Review Activity Planner and Activity Counter.**

3. **Check for problems and problem-solve.**

4. **Reinforce the integration / link to daily tasks and routine.**

5. **Upgrade activities as appropriate.**

6. **Introduce an additional one to two balance and one to two strength activities.**

7. **Develop plans for embedding the activities into the participant's daily routine.**

8. **Complete or have the participant complete the Activity Planner and Activity Counter.**

9. **Wrap up / review session.**

1. Review the balance and strength activities commenced previously

The participant should demonstrate the activities introduced at the previous session. Therapist should:

- correct any technique problems
- reinforce the balance and strength principles as you review the activities with the participant
- assess how and where the participant has integrated the balance and strength activities into their daily routine. Look at whether they have changed any routines or moved any household objects to act as a prompt to doing the LiFE activity and to facilitate the activity becoming habitual
- provide positive reinforcement if the participants have done activities
- problem-solve if participants have experienced any difficulties.

The therapist should check for any problems and should judge how effectively the participant is integrating or embedding the activities into their daily routine.

2. Review Activity Planner and Activity Counter

These records are a useful tool to indicate problems that participants may have with the activities. They also work as a powerful reinforcer of the activities. For a number of reasons, it is recommended that these records are consulted at every visit. These reasons include:

- to determine how frequently the participant has been doing the activities
- to examine whether participants were able to achieve the goals they set the previous session
- to determine if there are any activities that the participant may be having problems with and to ascertain the reason(s) why
- to act as a motivational tool.

Many people find these sheets difficult to fill in initially. The therapist should strongly encourage the participant to continue filling in the sheets as they are a valuable learning tool.

If the participant was able to successfully achieve their goal they should receive positive feedback. They should be encouraged to set new, more challenging goals.

See the section on the activity recording sheets for complete instructions and rationale behind keeping these records.

3. Check for problems and problem-solve

Discuss with the participant any problems they may have encountered. These may include, but not be limited to:

- activities taught in the previous or any earlier sessions
- difficulties embedding the activities into daily routine
- performance of specific activities
- upgrading activities.

If participants were not able to achieve a set goal, review why they could not achieve it. Work together to determine why they were not able to achieve it and attempt to set a more realistic goal. Problem-solve collaboratively to resolve any difficulties encountered. Gradually try to increase the autonomy of the participant in problem solving. An example of this could be the participant not remembering to do the activity. As the therapist, you might like to ask things such as: 'Why do you think you couldn't remember? Were you able to do it and couldn't remember or you were unable to do the activity? Would it help to do the activity and just not do the recording?' Encourage and facilitate having the participant work out the problem and the solution. Provide praise and positive reinforcement for any activities that they have done no matter how few. Encourage them to build on any level of achievement. Remember that the participant may need more than one prompt to problem-solve.

4. Reinforce the integration / link to daily tasks and routine

Check how, when and where the participant has integrated the balance and strength activities since the previous session. Look at whether they have moved any household objects to act as a prompt to doing the LiFE activity. This will facilitate the activity becoming habitual. Provide positive feedback when they have made changes to facilitate the activities becoming habitual.

If the participant is having difficulties linking activities to their daily routine, you may be able to suggest other cues. Other cues may be linking the LiFE activity to a particular situation or context. Look for places and tasks in the participant's daily routine where the LiFE activities can be embedded. Try to encourage the participant to link the LiFE activities with their usual daily activities.

5. Upgrade activities as appropriate

As you check the activities done since the last session you should encourage the participant to upgrade any activities that they have mastered. You may need to demonstrate ways that they can do this appropriately and safely. Upgrades should be recorded on the activity recording sheets.

There is more information on upgrading activities in the sections on teaching the balance and strength activities.

6. Introduce an additional one to two balance and one to two strength activities

There is no specific order in which the activities must be implemented. It is best to start with activities that the participant will be able to perform so that they can achieve the goals that they set. Work towards the activities that the participant may find most challenging. The activities do not need to be done in the order that they are presented in the manual. The goal is to have all activities completed by the end of training.

Participants should be able to introduce at least one to two balance and one to two strength activities each session. The format of five sessions is based on the participant being able to manage an additional two balance and two strength activities each week. If they cannot they will require more sessions than is listed in the research format.

7. Develop plans for embedding the activities into the participant's daily routine.

Participants need to plan how they will embed the newly learned activities into their routine. They should also include plans to keep doing activities that have been previously learned. Throughout these sessions the participant should gradually increase the amount of control they have over setting these goals and embedding these activities.

See section on 'Planning and recording performance of the LiFE activities' for examples of this.

8. Complete or have the participant complete the Activity Planner and Activity Counter

Initially the therapist might complete or assist the participant in completing the sheets. However, participants should gradually take over the task of planning where they will embed the activities and filling in the activity recording sheets with the goals for the following week or weeks. It can be helpful to have participants articulate their plan for embedding activities while the therapist is there.

At the end of each session the therapist should ensure that the participant has a sufficient number of recording sheets to last until the next session.

9. Wrap up / review session

Before leaving, check again if there is anything that participants would like clarified. Briefly go over what has been covered in the session. Ensure that participants understand what is expected of them between sessions and when the next therapist visit is scheduled. Usually the following visit is booked with the participant at this time.

Throughout each session

Throughout each session, engage participants in planning how, when and where activities will be embedded and how they will upgrade activities. You will need to provide positive reinforcement and encouragement. This is integral to the role the therapist has and should be provided in each and every session. It is not a separate activity but flows from the positive dialogue that the therapist needs to develop with each participant. Finally, the trainer needs to check the safety of the participant. Safety is paramount to the program and participants should be reminded that each activity they perform should be performed safely. It is particularly important to reinforce this when participants are upgrading their activities: participants are encouraged to challenge themselves but to keep safety in mind at all times.

Sessions 6 and 7 (booster sessions)

If the participant has been able to learn all the activities and integrate them into their daily routines by session 5, then sessions 6 and 7 may be used to reinforce the program and to check on the progress and safety the of participant as required.

Session 6 should be conducted after at least a two-week break following session 5. Session 7 should then follow approximately four weeks after session 6. These breaks allow the therapist and the participant to evaluate how the participant is managing independently.

Although a timeframe of eight to twelve weeks is suggested to implement these final two sessions, this should be seen as a guideline (refer to Table 1 for the timing of sessions).The scheduling will depend on the needs of the participant.

Some participants may not have been able to learn and integrate all the activities by session 5. In this case the therapist may use sessions 6 and 7 to continue teaching and implementing the activities. This is done in the same manner as the previous sessions.

The aims, objectives and components of sessions 6 and 7 are in line with sessions 2–5. However by the end of session 7 participants should be fully autonomous in embedding, performing and upgrading the activities in the LiFE program.

An additional component for these final two sessions is to:

Finalise the implementation of the LiFE program

These sessions should provide an opportunity to reinforce the key points, principles and activities of the LiFE program. Participants should be encouraged to try to embed and perform all the activities in the program. The ones they find most challenging may be the ones that they most need to practise.

The therapist and participant can review how the participant has managed to implement the program and address any issues that may have arisen.

Participants should be reminded that this is a lifestyle program and that they should continue to challenge themselves and upgrade their activities on their own on an ongoing basis.

Phone calls

Phone calls to the participants are used as an adjunct to the teaching sessions. The timing is designed to provide a reminder to the participants to continue to do the activities. As a guide we suggest that calls to the participants be made at approximately weeks 10 and 20. However, this may vary depending on how confident the therapist is that the participant is able to manage independently.

The first phone call is scheduled to be a couple of weeks after the first booster session (session 6). This is to allow the participant the opportunity to have been working independently on embedding all the activities into their daily routine. By scheduling it before the next booster session (session 7) it allows the therapist to determine what might need to be covered in the subsequent booster session.

The second call is scheduled to be a reasonable length of time after the participant has been managing the program independently.

The purpose of the telephone calls is to provide an opportunity to:

- Discuss any difficulties participants may be having with the program and to provide a sounding board for them to problem-solve.
- Discuss changes participants have made to their day in order to incorporate the balance and strength activities.
- Discuss upgrading activities with participants to keep them challenging themselves.
- Reinforce the principles of the LiFE program.
- Encourage and motivate participants to continue with the program and to be more active.

LiFE

Planning and recording performance of the LiFE activities

Planning and recording performance of the LiFE activities

Planning and recording

There are two types of planning and recording sheets used in the LiFE program. These are the Activity Planner and the Activity Counter. Participants need to be taught how to fill in these forms. They also need to understand the rationale for completing them. The purpose of completing these sheets is to help plan the activities to be performed and to help the participant to remember to perform the activities in the program. Filling in the forms assists in taking the activity from something that participants have to consciously think about to something that becomes habitual.

Activity Planner

The Activity Planner is a tool that has a dual role. It is used to help particpants plan what they intend to do. It also records what they have been able to do and this provides feedback to both them and the therapist about the performance of the activities. The Activity Planner helps participants make the activities habitual and encourages them to look for opportunities in their daily routine where LiFE activities can be embedded.

The rationale behind completing the Activity Planner is that it:

- assists the participants to visualise the activities and plan how, when and where they will embed and perform the activities
- reminds participants to do the activities
- reinforces the performance of the activities
- helps established the habit of performing the activities
- helps the participant to learn all the activities
- indicates to the therapist with which activities the participant may be having problems.

There is one sheet for balance activities and one for strength activities. They are filled in daily, either as the participant performs the activity or at the end of the day. The purpose of this form is to record if the participant has done that particular activity on that particular day. It is not to count the number of times each day the participant has performed the activity. If they have done the activity it is like ticking off an item on a 'to do' list. This provides positive reinforcement. If they have not remembered to do a particular activity they will be reminded to do it the following day. The focus of the Activity Planner is on having remembered to do the activity, not the number of times the activity was performed.

> **The LiFE Activity Planner and an example of a completed LiFE Activity Planner can be found on the following pages. It can also be downloaded from the Sydney University Press website at purl.library.usyd.edu.au/sup/9781743320372.**

LIFE Activity Planner: balance training. Week starting   /   /

Balance principle	Balance activity	Example of daily tasks. How, when and where?	Tick if done							
Decrease base of support	Tandem stand									
	Tandem walk									
	One-leg stand									
Shifting weight and moving to the limits of stability	Leaning side to side									
	Leaning forwards and backwards									
Stepping over objects	Stepping forwards and backwards									
	Stepping side to side									

lIFE Activity Planner: strength training. Week starting / /

Strength principle	Strength activity	Example of daily tasks. How, when and where?	Tick if done							
Bend your knees	Bend knees									
Sit to stand	Normal chair									
	Low chair									
On your toes	Stand on toes									
	Walk on toes									
On your heels	Stand on Heels									
	Walk on heels									
Up the stairs	Up stairs									
Move sideways	Step sideways									
Tighten muscles	Move Ankles									
	Bend / straighten knees									
	Tighten / relax buttocks									

How to complete the Activity Planner

Adding the day / date

This is the blank box just below 'tick if done'.

The forms have been designed to be completed over a seven-day period. The first set should have the day / date filled in by the therapist. For example, if your initial session with the participant is on a Tuesday the recording should start either on that day or the following day and should be filled in for the next seven days. If you will not be seeing the participant one week from commencement you should leave them with enough day / date filled forms for each day until you next meet.

Example of daily task: linking the activities to and embedding them within daily tasks

This section is for participants to write which daily task they plan to embed the activity into and when they plan to do it. It helps visualise how and plan when they will do the activity. The task becomes the reminder to do the balance or strength activity.

This section should initially be filled in by the therapist. At the first training session fill out an example of a task the participant is going to link the balance or strength activity to. Using the participant's completed Daily Routine Chart as a prompt, engage the participant in coming up with their own ideas for appropriate daily tasks in which to embed the activities.

For example, the participant might say that they brush their teeth morning and night. You might suggest that this is a good time to do a balance activity such as standing on one leg with an appropriate level of support. Brushing their teeth then becomes the prompt or reminder to do the balance activity.

Initially the participant will need some help in order to come up with daily tasks into which activities can be embedded. However, as they become familiar with the activities they should gradually take over the role of deciding to what tasks an activity will be connected. Encourage the participant to come up with their own ideas and emphasise that this is their program and that the more that they put into it the more they will get out of it. If they are unsure of a certain situation and if it would be appropriate to embed an activity into it, they should to discuss the idea with you first.

Monday

LiFE Activity Planner: balance training. Week starting 3/2/14

Balance principle	Balance activity	Example of daily tasks. How, when and where?	Tick if done						
			MON 3/2	TUES 4/2	WED 5/2	THURS 6/2	FRI 7/2	SAT 8/2	SUN 9/2
Decrease base of support	Tandem stand	At the kitchen sink when washing up	✓	not wash	✓	✓	✓	not wash	✓
	Tandem walk	Along the hallway (kitchen to loungeroom) after dinner (going to watch TV)			✓	✓	✓	✓	✓
	One-leg stand	While brushing my teeth – morning + night – alternate legs.	✓	✓	✓	✓	✓	✓	✓
Shifting weight and moving to the limits of stability	Leaning side to side	While blowdrying my hair after washing +/or while brushing it at night.	✓		✓	✓	✓	✓	
	Leaning forwards and backwards								
Stepping over objects	Stepping forwards and backwards	Over the "lip" of the tiles when going into the laundry to iron clothes in the morning.	✓	✓	✓	✓	✓	✓	✓
	Stepping side to side								

LiFE Activity Planner: strength training. Week starting 3/2/14

Mon

Strength principle	Strength activity	Example of daily tasks. How, when and where?	Tick if done			
			MON	WED	FRI	SUN
Bend your knees	Bend knees	When unloading the dishwasher. Getting pegs out of peg basket.	✓	✓	✓	✓
Sit to stand	Normal chair					
	Low chair	When I get off/out of the lounge after watching TV at night.	✓	✓	✓	✓
On your toes	Stand on toes	Each time I get the cups out of the cupboard.	✓	✓	✓	✓
	Walk on toes	Down the hallway to the laundry to iron or wash.	✓	✓	✓	✓
On your heels	Stand on Heels					
	Walk on heels	Along the hallway back from the laundry.	✓	✓	✓	
Up the stairs	Up stairs	Every time I need to take something to bedrooms/bathrooms upstairs.				
Move sideways	Step sideways	When walking beside the car in the garage before I get in to drive.	✓	✓	✓	✓
Tighten muscles	Move Ankles	During the ad breaks	✓	✓	✓	✓
	Bend / straighten knees	while watching TV at night.	✓	✓	✓	✓
	Tighten / relax buttocks	night.	✓	✓	✓	✓

Ticking the boxes: activity performance

The participant completes the form by ticking the box each day of the week that they have remembered to do each balance and strength activity. On these forms they do not need to record the number of times that they perform the activity, just that they have done the activity at least once during that particular day. However, participants should be encouraged to do the activities more than once during the day. They should try to link the activity to a daily task. Linking the activity to a daily task acts as a reminder to do the activity.

The participant can either complete the form at a particular time of the day, such as just after dinner, or they can do it during the day as they have done that particular activity. (See example for completed form.)

Reviewing the Activity Planner

These sheets are designed to assist in planning and reinforcing the activities. They also provide feedback to the therapist and the participant about the participant's ability to perform the activity. The information on the sheets may indicate if the participant is having any difficulties that require therapist assistance.

Reviewing the sheets at each session reinforces the importance of completing them. Completing them reinforces the performance of the activities.

Activity Counter

This form is for participants to record the **number** of times that they perform a particular activity on a specified day. Counting acts as a reinforcer for the activity. It establishes a baseline from which participants can measure their own improvement or achievement and provides an incentive to increase the number of times an activity is performed.

It would not be possible to count every activity every day. As a sample, though, it was decided to get participants to count the activities they do on two days per week. As a general rule, one of these days is used to count the number of balance activities performed and the other day is used to count the number of strength activities performed.

> **The LiFE Activity Counter and an example of a completed LiFE Activity Counter can be found on the following pages. It can also be downloaded from the Sydney University Press website at purl.library.usyd.edu.au/sup/9781743320372.**

LIFE Activity Counter. Week starting: / /

Activity	Day	Count

Have you had any problems while doing any of the activities in this program?

Yes / No

If yes, please give details

liFE Activity Counter. Week starting: 3 / 2 / 14.

Activity	Day	Count
Single leg stand	Tuesday	
Bend the knees .	Thursday	

Have you had any problems while doing any of the activities in this program?

Yes / No

If yes, please give details

How to complete the Activity Counter

Initially the therapist chooses two activities – one for balance and one for strength – that the participant will count in the following week. These are recorded on the form.

Have the participant choose the two days where they will count the activities performed. Record the chosen days on the form. A good idea initially is to count on days where the participant knows that they will be at home for a large part of the day. This can change as the participant becomes more familiar with the process. The days chosen to count do not have to be the same each week. It is better if they are not consecutive days though this is not essential. Each week a different balance and strength activity is recorded.

There were many participants who found counting helpful, especially in the early stages. However, there were some who were not compliant with this activity. We have included it as it was quite a strong reinforcer for many of the participants once they understood the importance.

Methods of counting

All participants were encouraged to count the specified activities and record the counting on the Activity Counter. There were a number of methods of counting that were used by the participants. These are outlined below. The preferred method for the research was the tally counter. However, not everyone wanted to use the tally counter. As the purpose of counting was to reinforce the activity, participants can choose the method which most suits them. The number they have counted is then recorded on the Activity Planner and Activity Counter.

Tally counter

During the research some of the participants used a tally counter (a clicker-style counter). Each time they performed the activity they 'clicked' and it kept count of the number. Participants were encouraged to keep the counter in a pocket or a conspicuous place like the kitchen bench. The participants needed to be taught how to use this device.

Example of tally counter.

Pen and paper recording

Some participants preferred to use pen and paper to record the number of times they performed the specified activities. Most just gave themselves a 'tick' each time they did the activity and recorded the number at the end of the day.

Estimating

There were some participants who preferred to estimate the number of times they performed the specified activity. This is the least ideal method, but can still be used as a reinforcer.

How to count the activities

It is important to remember that the 'number' participants have to better is specific to their particular circumstances. Their program is unique to them, their surroundings and their daily routine. A set of stairs for one participant may be the five stairs at the back door. For another participant it may be fifteen stairs to the upper level of their house.

Walking activities

The walking activities should be counted per episode. For example, if the participant tandem walks along the hallway, this would be counted as one episode. If they walked back again that would count as another episode. Walking activities would include tandem walking, sideways walking, walking on toes and walking on heels.

Leaning: forwards and backwards, side to side

Leaning to the left and then to the right is counted as one. Leaning forwards and then backwards is counted as one.

Stepping over objects: forwards and backwards, side to side

The participant must step forwards and then backwards to record this as one. The participant must step sideways over the object and then step back to the other side for a count of one.

Sit to stand

Standing up from a seated position counts as one. Reinforce to the participant that they must think about thow they are getting out of the chair, using as little support from their hands as possible.

Up the stairs

The number of stairs available to each participant will vary. The idea is to encourage the participants to take the stairs more often, rather than avoiding them, and for participants to concentrate on using their legs to go up the stairs rather than to rely on pulling with their arms. Participants should use whatever number of steps they have in their home as the count of one.

Emphasise to the participant that by practising the activities and by completing the activity forms daily, this is helping to reinforce the activities and to form new routines and eventually new habits for life.

Final note

The LiFE trainer's manual is designed to be used in conjunction with the LiFE participant's manual. Therapists should have read the participant's manual thoroughly and need to have incorporated at least some of the LiFE activities into their own lives before teaching them to participants.

Trainers should read the 'Stories and quotes' section of the participant's manual. This will help them to understand some of the positive outcomes achieved with the program and provide stories to share with their participants.

It is important that trainers have some understanding of habit formation, gait and gait patterns and other falls prevention exercise programs.

References

References

Anstey, K. J., Burns, R., von Sanden, C., Luszcz, M. A., Anstey, K. J., Burns, R., Luszcz, M. A. (2008). Psychological well-being is an independent predictor of falling in an 8-year follow-up of older adults. *Journals of Gerontology Series B-Psychological Sciences & Social Sciences, 63*(4), 249–257.

Bandura, A. (1997). *Self-efficacy: the exercise of control.* New York: W.H. Freeman.

Beauchet, O., Annweiler, C., Allali, G., Berrut, G., Herrmann, F. R., & Dubost, V. (2008). Recurrent falls and dual task-related decrease in walking speed: is there a relationship? *Journal of the American Geriatrics Society, 56*(7), 1265–1269.

Clemson, L., Fiatarone Singh, M., Bundy, A., Cumming, R. G., Manollaras, K., O'Loughlin, P., & Black, D. (2012). Integration of balance and strength training into daily life activity to reduce rate of falls in older people (the LiFE study): randomised parallel trial. *British Medical Journal, 345*:e4547.

Clemson, L., Fiatarone Singh, M., Bundy, A. C., Cumming, R. G., Weissel, E., Munro, J., Black, D. (2010). LiFE pilot study: a randomised trial of balance and strength training embedded in daily life activity to reduce falls in older adults. *Australian Occupational Therapy Journal, 57*(1), 42–50.

Clemson, L., & Swann, M. (2008). *Stepping on: building confidence and reducing falls. A community based program for older people* (2nd ed.). Camperdown, NSW: Sydney University Press.

Fiatarone Singh, M. A., & Murphy, K. (2003). *Helping elders activate their lives. HEAL program training manual for staff and exercise leaders.* Boston: Hebrew Rehabilitation Center for the Aged & Fit forYour Life Foundation, Ltd.

Friery, L. (2007). *Rasch analysis of the LiFE assessment of functional balance and strength.* Lidcombe: The University of Sydney.

Holland, R. W., Aarts, B., & Langendam, D. (2006). Breaking and creating habits on the working floor: a field-experiment on the power of implementation intentions. *Journal of Experimental Social Psychology, 42,* 776–783.

Kuptniratsaikul, V., Praditsuwan, R., Assantachai, P., Ploypetch, T., Udompunturak, S., & Pooliam, J. (2011). Effectiveness of simple balancing training program in elderly patients with history of frequent falls. *Clinical Interventions in Aging, 6,*111–117. *Epub 2011 May 6.*

Lally, P., & Gardner, B. (2011). Promoting habit formation. *Health Psychology Review.* doi: 10.1080/17437199.2011.603640

Liu-Ambrose, T., Ahamed, Y., Graf, P., Feldman, F., & Robinovitch, S. N. (2008). Older fallers with poor working memory overestimate their postural limits. *Archives of Physical Medicine and Rehabilitation, 89*(7), 1335–1340.

Lord, S. R., Sherrington, C., & Menz, H. B. (2001). *Falls in older people: risk factors and strategies for prevention*. Cambridge: Cambridge University Press.

Ronis, D. L., Yates, J. F., & Kirscht, J. P. (1989). Attitudes, decisions, and habits as determinants of repeated behavior. In A. R. Pratkanis, S. J. Breckler & A. G. Greenwald (eds), *Attitude, structure and function* (pp. 213–239). NY: Erlbaum.

Silsupadol, P., Lugade, V., Shumway-Cook, A., van Donkelaar, P., Chou, L.-S., Mayr, U., & Woollacott, M. H. (2009). Training-related changes in dual-task walking performance of elderly persons with balance impairment: a double-blind, randomized controlled trial. *Gait & Posture, 29*(4), 634–639.

Whittle, M. (1991). *Gait analysis: an introduction*. Oxford: Butterworth–Heinemann.

Index

Index

A

Activity Counter 42, 62, 65, 68, 80
  Activity Counter sheet 81
Activity Planner 42, 62, 65, 68, 73–77
  Activity Planner balance training sheet 75
  Activity Planner strength training sheet 76
assessing the ability of participants 23
autonomy of participants 18

B

balance training
  activities 3
  challenging balance 6, 13, 49
  correct performance of balance activities 8
  principles of 3, 44, 61
  upgrading balance activities 50
base of support 44. *See also* support, reducing your base of; *See also* safety
'bend your knees' activity 52

C

checking up on the participant 9
  phone calls 70
  recording the progress of participants 62
  reviewing activities 65
combining activities 49. *See also* upgrading activities

D

Daily Routine Chart (DRC) 23–25, 41, 59
  DRC sheet 25
demonstrating the activities 41
dorsiflexors, strengthening of 19, 54, 55

E

encouragement 42
executive function 13
expectations of participants 7

F

falls prevention 3–4, 10, 13, 19, 85
functional exercise 3, 12
functional plasticity 13

G

gait 13, 19, 85
goals 63

H

habits, forming good 6, 10, 15–18, 73, 85
Helping Elders Activate their Lives (HEAL) 3

I

incorporating activities into daily life 3, 6, 12, 14, 66, 77
  cues 43

L

leaning activities
  'leaning forwards and backwards' activity 46, 84
  'leaning from side to side' activity 46, 84
LiFE Assessment Tool (LAT) 26–37, 60
  grading levels 27–28
  LAT balance activities sheet 30–31
  LAT balance and strength assessment sheet 26, 30, 32
  LAT strength activities sheet 32–33
LiFE principles 3, 10, 41
Lifestyle-integrated Functional Exercise (LiFE) program to prevent falls: participant's manual 5, 41, 60, 85

M

moving slowly 51
multitasking 49

O

'one-leg stand' activity 45
'on your heels' activities 54
'on your toes' activities 53

P

participant's manual. *See Lifestyle-integrated Functional Exercise (LiFE) program to prevent falls: participant's manual*
physical activity 6
plantarflexors, strengthening of 19, 53, 55
postural control 13

R

reinforcement 17, 42, 66, 73
repetition 17
routine 6

S

safety 6, 8, 14, 62
Short Portable Mental Status Questionnaire 11
'sit to stand' activities 52, 84
spatial processing 13
squats 6
stability, moving to the limits of 44, 46
'static balance' assessment tool 37
'stepping over objects' activities 44, 47, 84
  'forwards and backwards' 47
  'side to side' 48
strength training
  activities 3
  correct performance of strength activities 8
  principles of 3, 51, 61
  upgrading strength activities 56
structure of the LiFE program
  session 1 9, 59–65
  sessions 2–5 9, 64–70
  sessions 6 and 7 9, 69
success of the LiFE program 10–12
support, reducing your base of 44, 49

T

'tandem stand' activity 44, 45
'tandem walk' activity 13, 44, 45
task coordination 13
teaching the program
  later stages 42
  who can teach the LiFE program 4–5
'tighten muscles' activities 55
'timed get-up-and-go' assessment tool 37
'timed tandem walk' assessment tool 37

U

upgrading activities 18–19, 43, 56, 62, 64
'up the stairs' activity 54, 84

W

walking 84
  scanning ahead 19
'walk sideways' activity 55

Lightning Source UK Ltd.
Milton Keynes UK
UKOW06f1921230115

245010UK00001B/14/P